for Gretchen and Kevin

ACKNOWLEDGMENTS

I am grateful to Edward Lear, whose delightful, timeless, and thoroughly smile-provoking verse was so inspirational. I would like to thank my husband, David Cowan; Karen Hatt, Barbara Ensor, and Elissa Schappell, who remain constant and generous with their support; my children, Aidan and Olive, whose scowls and smiles help lead me in the right direction; and Anthony Accardi of Green Rhino Inc., who dared to teach an old dog some new and very useful tricks. And I am forever thankful to Lee Wade and Anne Schwartz, whose brilliance and banter make everything fun.

A NOTE ABOUT THE ART

I've enjoyed imagining that Mr. Lear used the word "old" as a term of endearment—rather than one reflecting age—when describing his friends the cake-lover from Rheims, the stilt-walker from Wilts, and others. My pictures reflect this.

Atheneum Books for Young Readers
An imprint of Simon & Schuster
Children's Publishing Division
1230 Avenue of the Americas
New York, New York 10020
Artwork copyright © 2004
by Valorie Ann Fisher
All rights reserved, including
the right of reproduction
in whole or in part in any form.

Book design by Lee Wade
Manufactured in China
First Edition
10 9 8 7 6 5 4 3 2 1
Library of Congress
Control Number:
2003010681
CIP data for this book is available
from the Library of Congress.
ISBN 0-689-86380-2

nonsense!

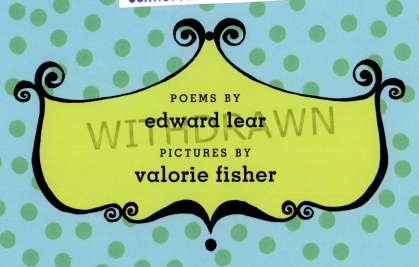

POEMS BY
edward lear

PICTURES BY
valorie fisher

AN ANNE SCHWARTZ BOOK

Atheneum Books for Young Readers

New York London Toronto Sydney

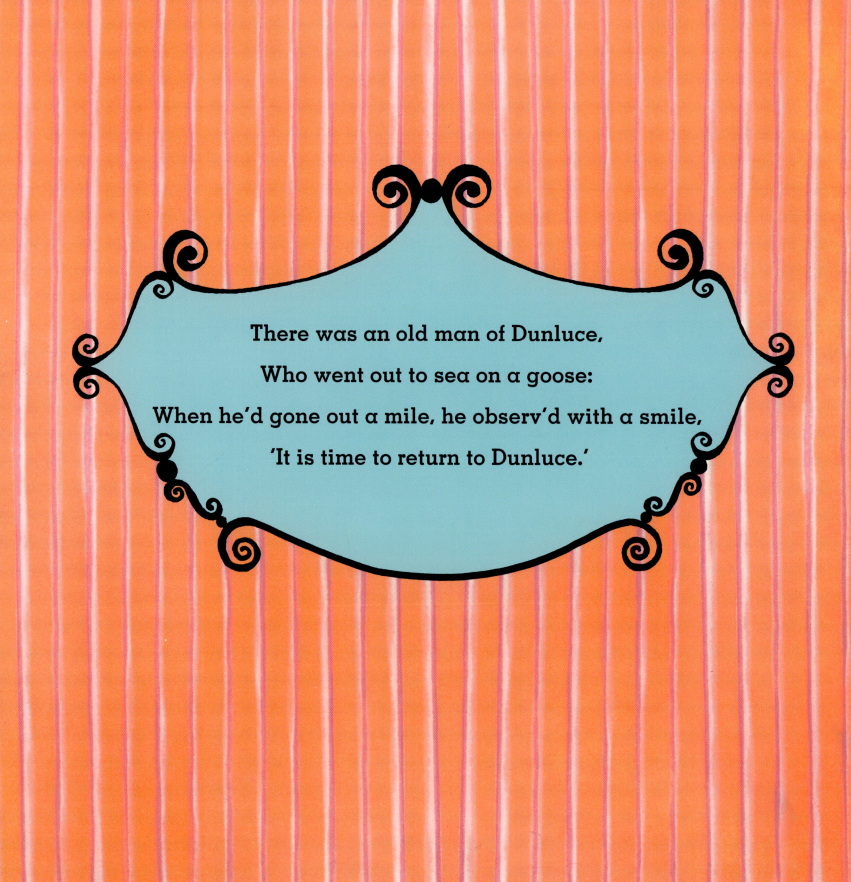

There was an old man of Dunluce,

Who went out to sea on a goose:

When he'd gone out a mile, he observ'd with a smile,

'It is time to return to Dunluce.'

There was a Young Lady of Welling,

Whose praise all the world was a telling;

She played on a harp, and caught several carp,

That accomplished Young Lady of Welling.

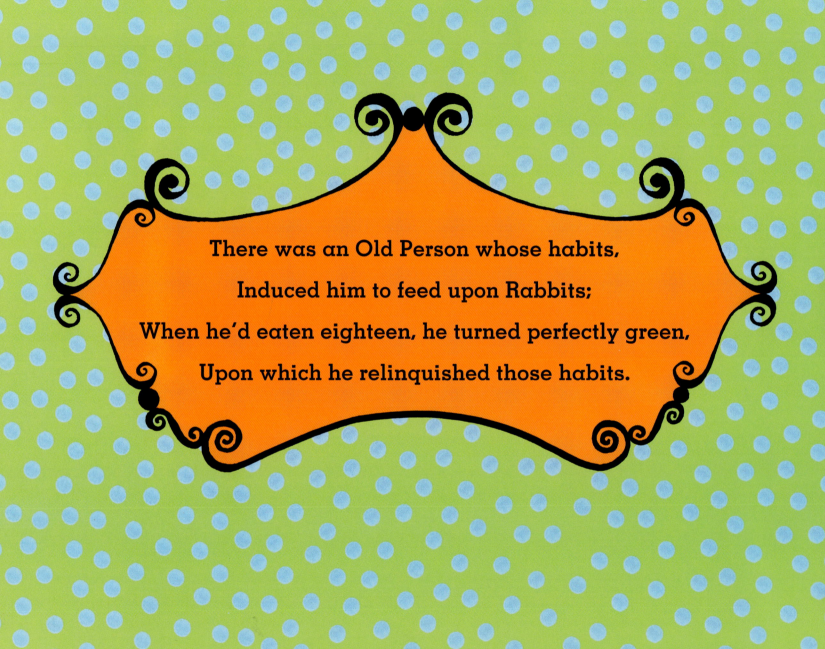

There was an Old Person whose habits,

Induced him to feed upon Rabbits;

When he'd eaten eighteen, he turned perfectly green,

Upon which he relinquished those habits.

There was an old man, who when little

Fell casually into a kettle;

But, growing too stout, he could never get out,

So he passed all his life in that kettle.

Home Sweet Home

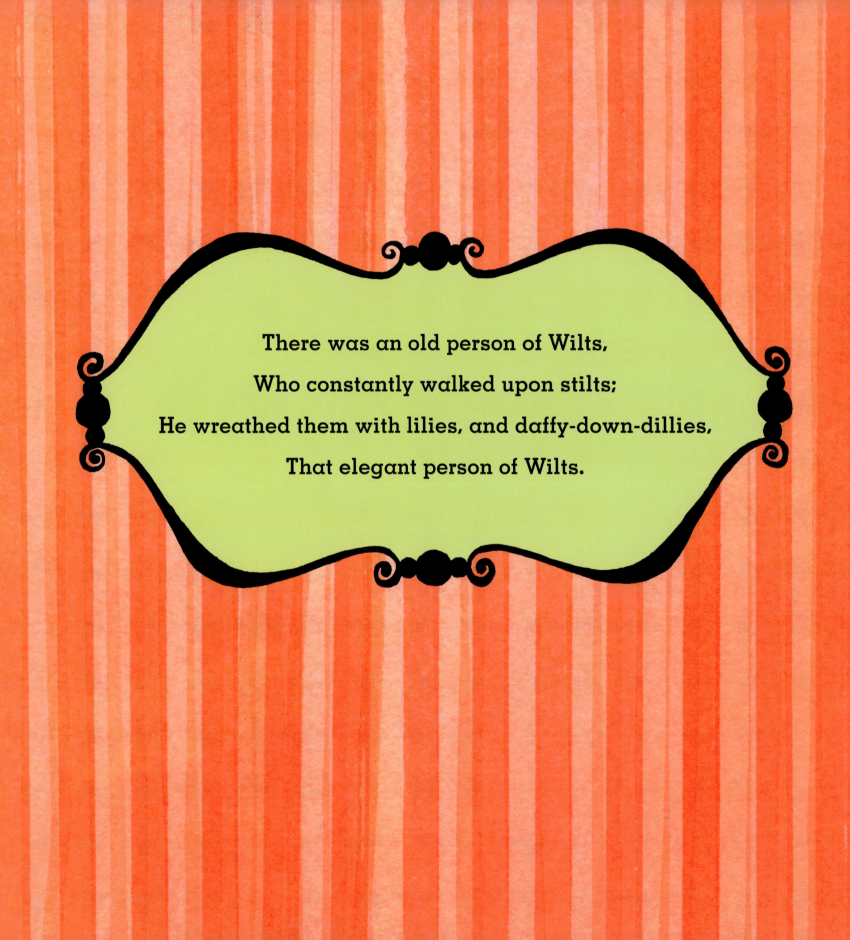

There was an old person of Wilts,

Who constantly walked upon stilts;

He wreathed them with lilies, and daffy-down-dillies,

That elegant person of Wilts.

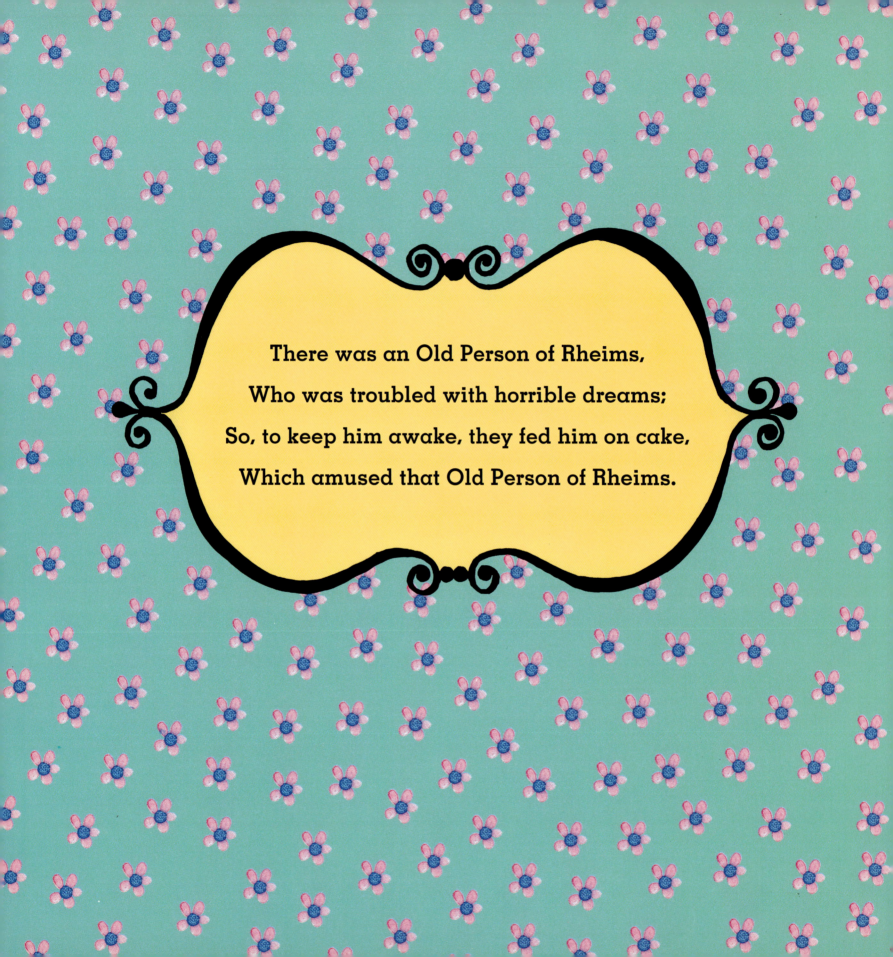

There was an Old Person of Rheims,

Who was troubled with horrible dreams;

So, to keep him awake, they fed him on cake,

Which amused that Old Person of Rheims.

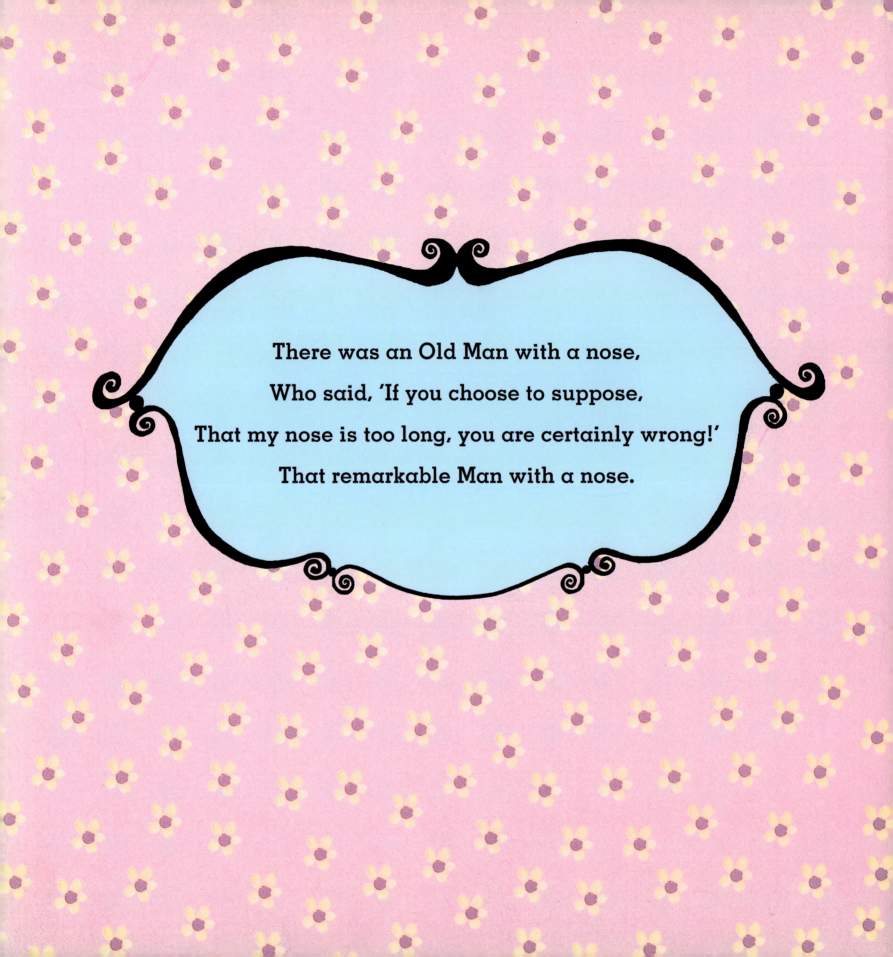

There was an Old Man with a nose,

Who said, 'If you choose to suppose,

That my nose is too long, you are certainly wrong!'

That remarkable Man with a nose.

Remarkable ∞ out of the ordinary

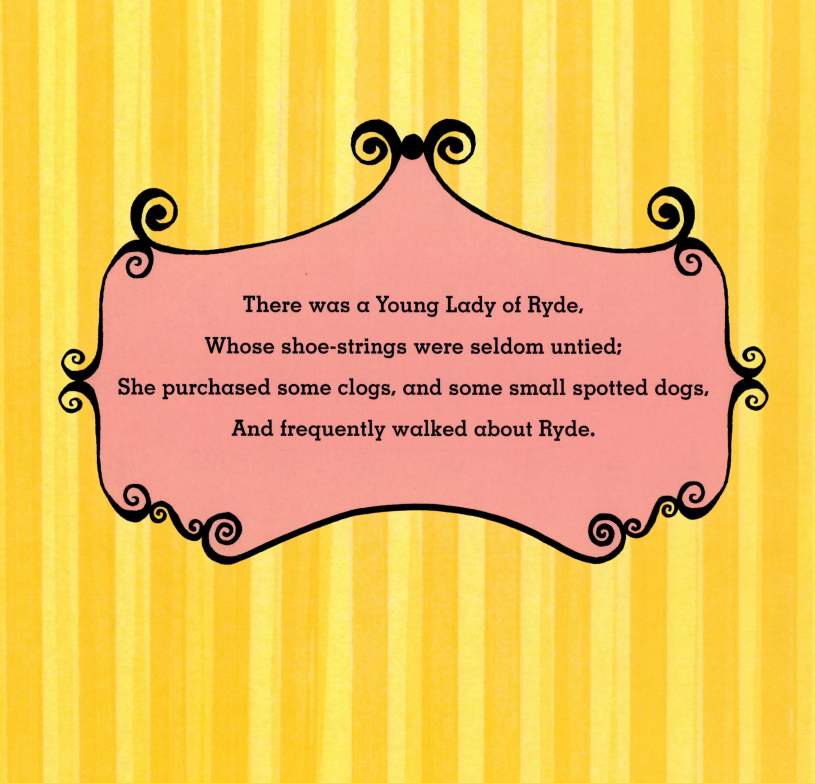

There was a Young Lady of Ryde,

Whose shoe-strings were seldom untied;

She purchased some clogs, and some small spotted dogs,

And frequently walked about Ryde.

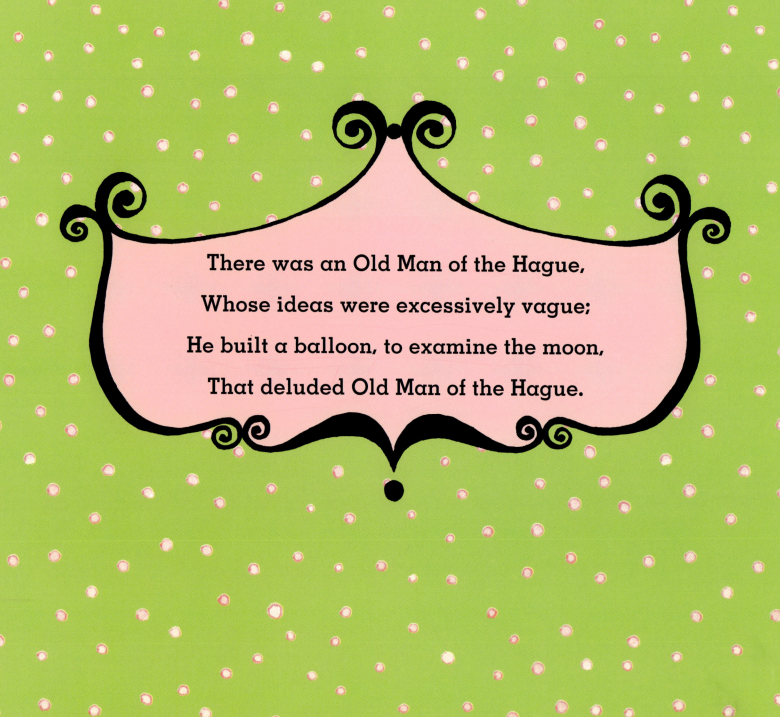

There was an Old Man of the Hague,

Whose ideas were excessively vague;

He built a balloon, to examine the moon,

That deluded Old Man of the Hague.

to delude: to trick the mind into believing something that perhaps is not true.

There was a young lady of Firle,

Whose hair was addicted to curl;

It curled up a tree, and all over the sea,

That expansive young lady of Firle.

ENGLISH CHANNEL

Expansive
1. tending to spread out.
2. generous & open with one's feelings.

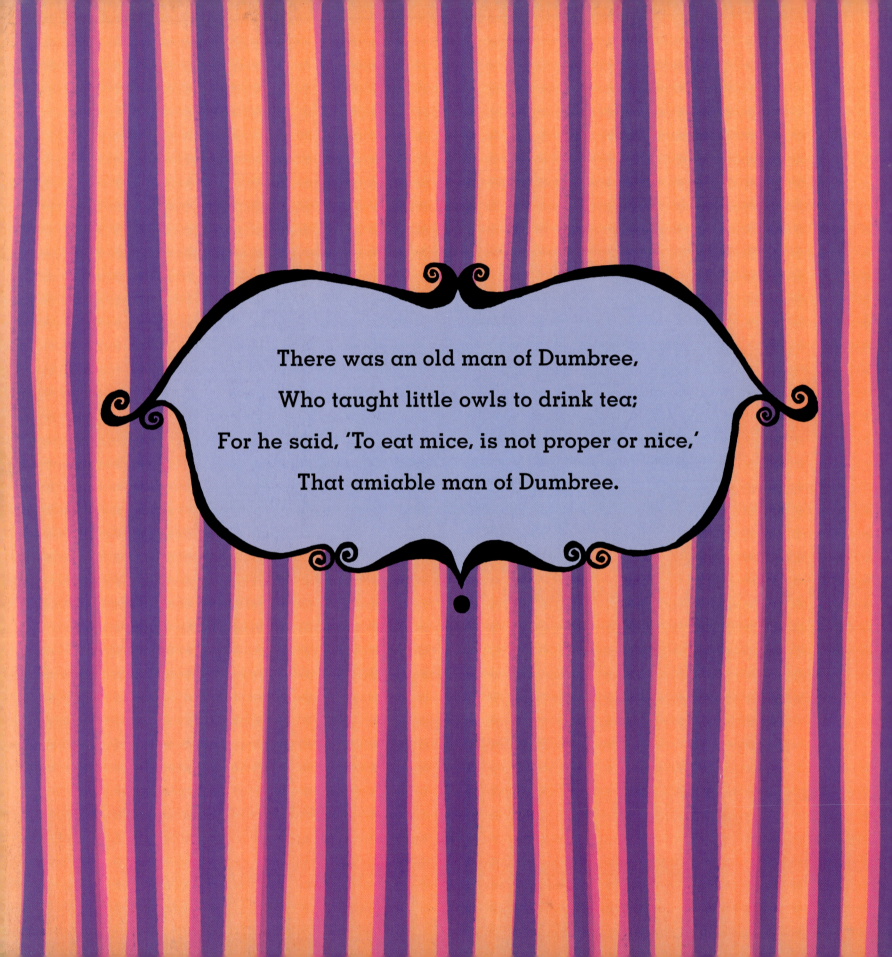

There was an old man of Dumbree,

Who taught little owls to drink tea;

For he said, 'To eat mice, is not proper or nice,'

That amiable man of Dumbree.

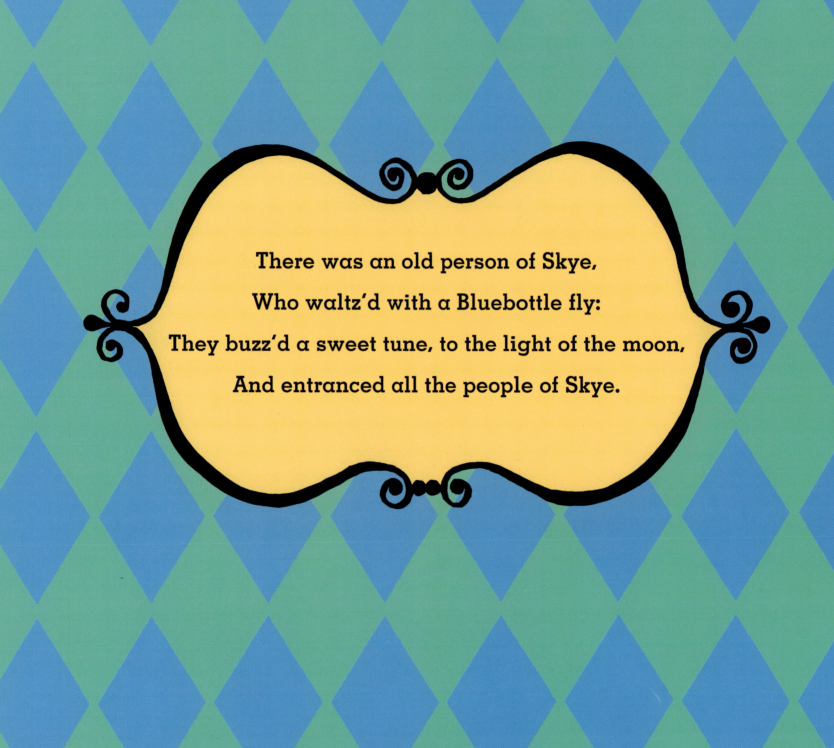

There was an old person of Skye,

Who waltz'd with a Bluebottle fly:

They buzz'd a sweet tune, to the light of the moon,

And entranced all the people of Skye.

Isle of Skye,
...⊙...
N.W.
Scotland

Entranced
...⊙...
filled with
delight and
wonder.

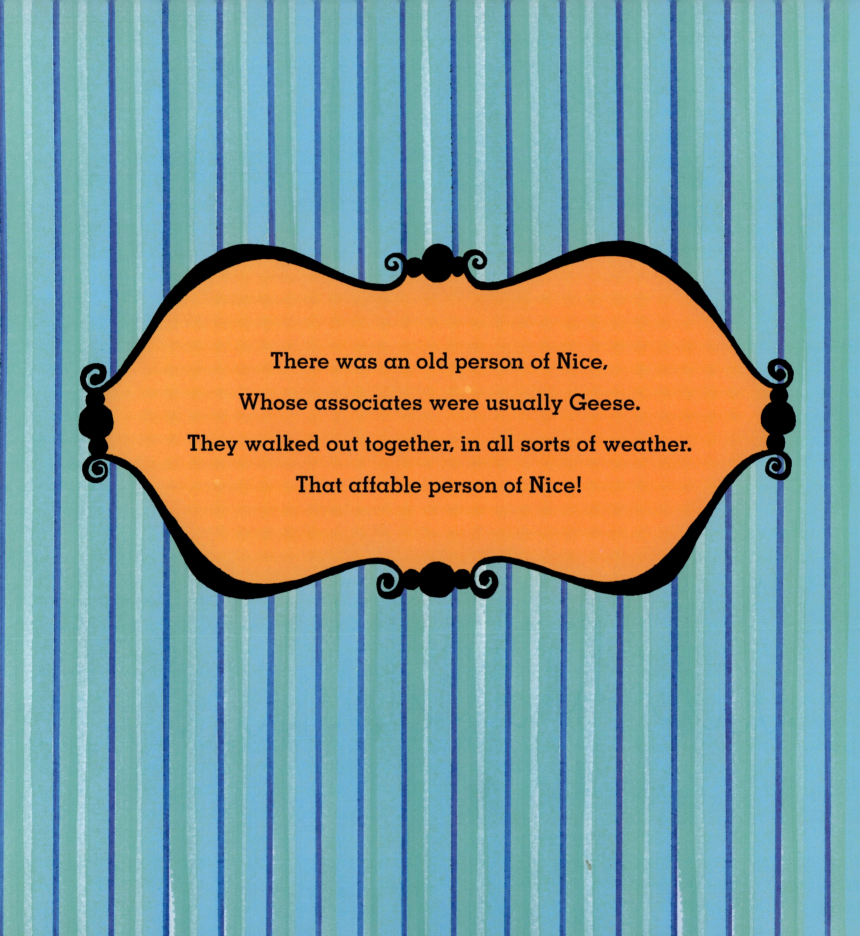

There was an old person of Nice,

Whose associates were usually Geese.

They walked out together, in all sorts of weather.

That affable person of Nice!

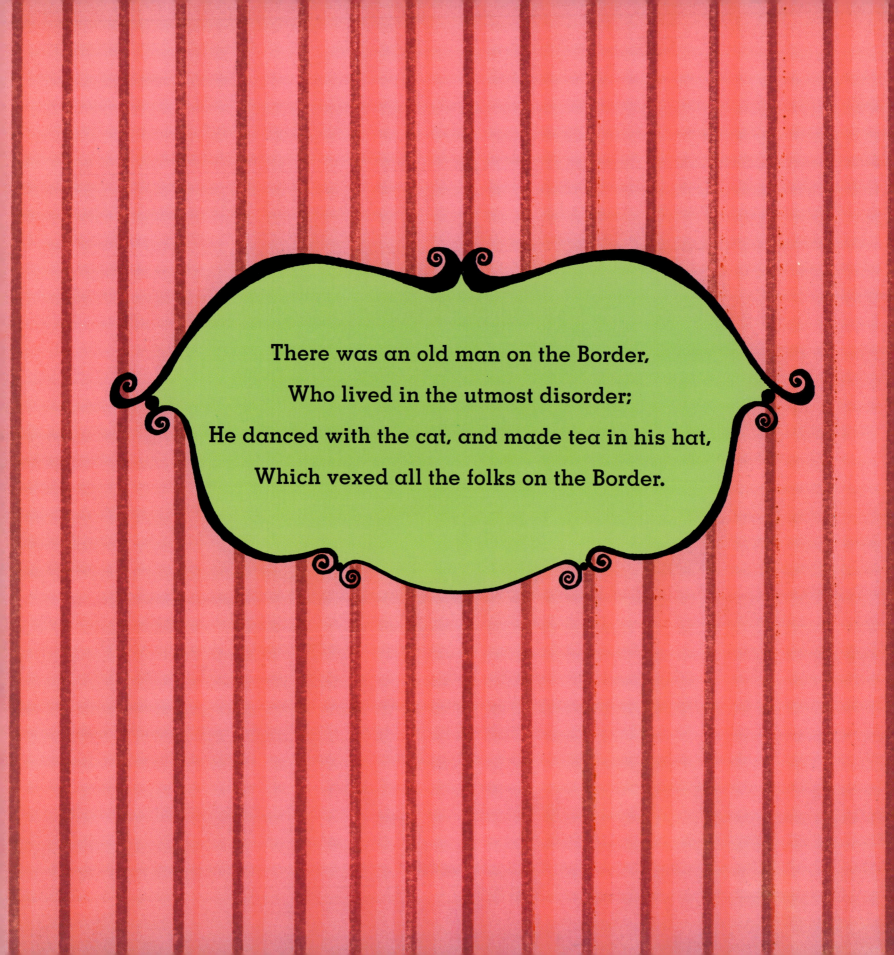

There was an old man on the Border,
Who lived in the utmost disorder;
He danced with the cat, and made tea in his hat,
Which vexed all the folks on the Border.

Vexed ❋ annoyed & irritated!

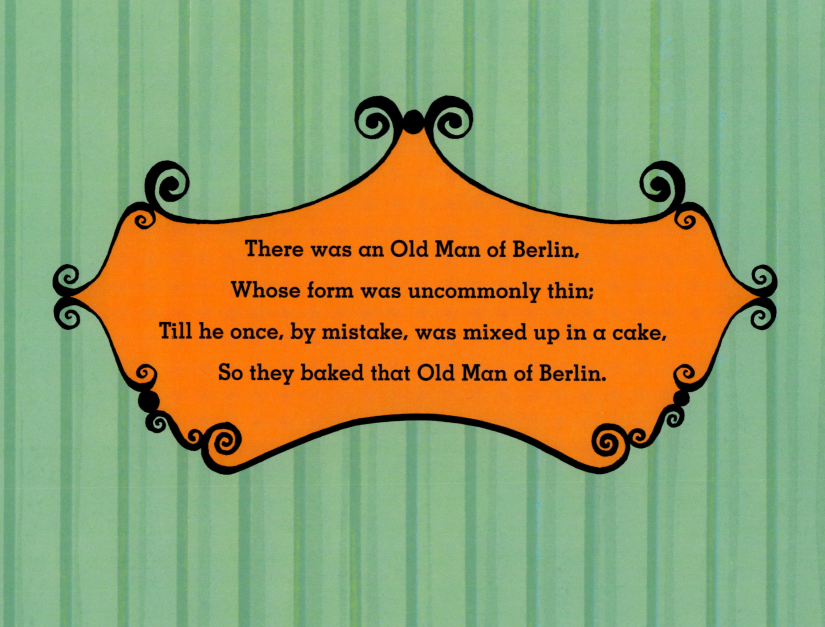

There was an Old Man of Berlin,

Whose form was uncommonly thin;

Till he once, by mistake, was mixed up in a cake,

So they baked that Old Man of Berlin.

ABOUT MR. LEAR

Edward Lear was born in England in 1812, the twentieth child in a family of twenty-one children. Lear's eldest sister, Ann, raised and educated him. As a child he loved to draw and was a gifted and natural talent. By the age of fifteen Lear was earning a living as an illustrator of birds and animals.

Lear's reputation as an accomplished artist grew. Queen Victoria was so impressed with his skills that she requested that he give her drawing lessons. The Earl of Derby, also a great admirer, commissioned Lear to draw all the birds and animals of the vast menagerie on his estate, Knowsley Hall. It was during this time that Lear began to write his wonderful nonsense poems to entertain all the children of Knowsley Hall. Fifteen years later he published those poems in *A Book of Nonsense* under the pseudonym Derry Down Derry. The nonsense poems became wildly popular and he went on to publish (using his real name) many more, including the much loved *The Owl and the Pussy-cat.*

Lear loved to travel and paint and spent most of his life doing just that. He traveled all over Europe and other faraway lands: Greece, Egypt, Israel, Jordan, and Lebanon. He finally settled in the coastal town of San Remo, Italy. Lear never married, but one of his dearest friends and constant companions was a cat named Old Foss. He died in 1888 at his home in San Remo.

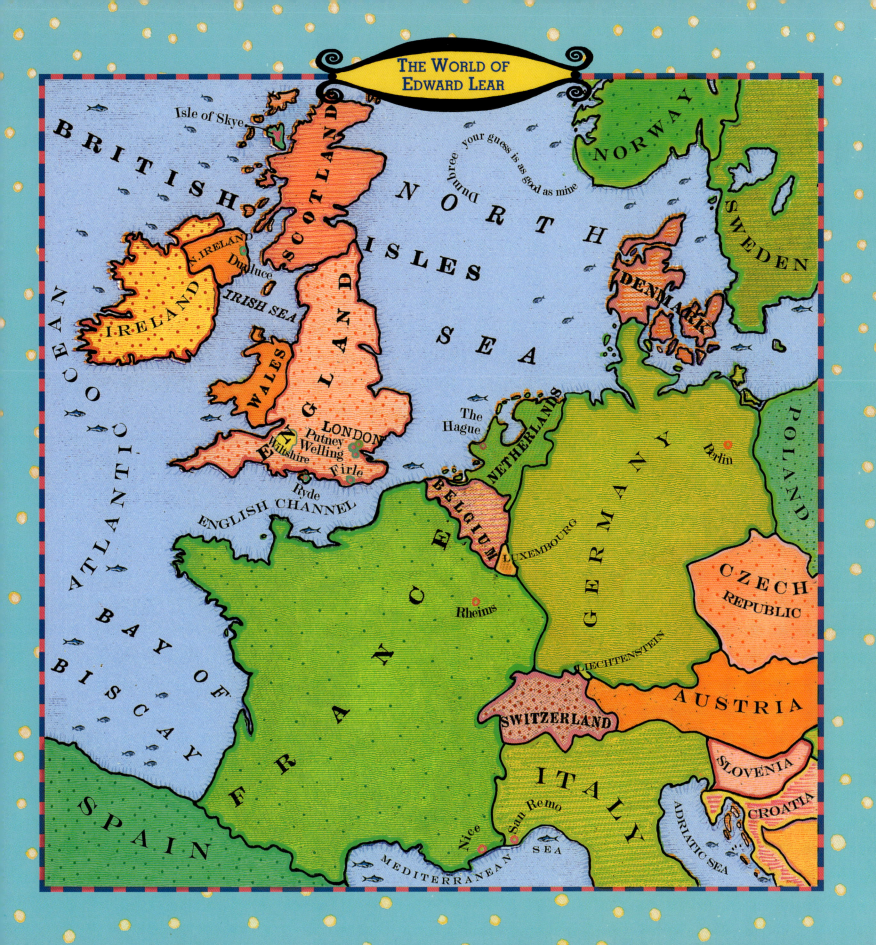